A Climber's Climber

On the Trail with Carl Blaurock

A Climber's Climber

On the Trail with Carl Blaurock

Edited by
Barbara J. Euser

With a Foreword by
David Lavender

CORDILLERA PRESS, INC.
Publishers in the Rockies

Library of Congress Cataloging in Publication Data

Blaurock, Carl, 1894-
  A climber's climber.

  Includes index.
  1. Blaurock, Carl, 1894- . 2. Mountaineers—
United States—Biography. 3. Mountaineering—United
States—History. I. Euser, Barbara J., 1949-
II. Title.
GV199.92.B59A33 1984 796.5'22'0924 (B) 84-9539

ISBN: 0-917895-01-0

First Edition

1 2 3 4 5 6 7 8 9

Printed in the United States of America

Acknowledgements

This book is the result of a partnership effort by many people. Editor Barb Euser deserves much credit for pursuing the idea of a book on Carl's adventures and for interviewing Carl and selecting many of the photographs. David Lavender delighted us with his enthusiasm for the project and his contribution of the foreword. Dave and Kip Shrum and their staff of Colorado Camera were patient and professional photographers when we arrived with Carl's treasured albums and instructions to "guard them with your lives." The Colorado Mountain Club supported the project with keen interest, and Carl has graciously donated his royalties from the book to the Colorado Mountain Club Foundation.

Our greatest debt, of course, is to Carl and Louise Blaurock, two charming people still so very much in love with each other after almost sixty years of marriage. Carl and Louise graciously opened their home to us and shared with us not only Carl's photographs and writings, but also their precious memories. May these pages relive those memories for Carl and Louise, just as they make us yearn to have shared the experiences with them.

The Publishers

Contents

Crestone Needle

A Special Voice

By David Lavender

One of the fine moments of campfire watching comes when the flames have dwindled to embers. When, after a moment of easy silence, a voice says, "Once upon a time" or "Way back when," and you know, sitting there in the soft darkness, that you are going to gain another bit of understanding about what makes mountaineering and the people you share it with what they are.

That is the kind of voice I heard when I read Carl Blaurock's reminiscences—"voice" in the sense of an authentic personality speaking through the print. Individuality. Truth. The campfires glowed again, and the years fell away, and for me it was 1927 once more.

My brother Dwight, who knew more about the Colorado Mountain Club and its members than I did, had made arrangements for us to join a group of them for a Fourth of July climb of Mount Wilson. Carl Blaurock, who I met then for the first time, and his husky sidekick, Bill Ervin, were the leaders. For reasons that elude me now, since I was a neophyte climber, I had an ice axe along. This gave me a place of honor near the front of the line, for there were not many such items on hand and occasional step cutting was necessary.

My vivid memory, though, is not of that slow labor, but of descending the long, steep tongues of snow that licked down into Navajo Basin. Carl, very bravely, introduced me to the glissade—leaning back, face forward, sliding ahead while using the axe as brake and rudder. He slid beside me a ways and then dropped off to help someone else, thinking perhaps I had caught the knack. Well, partly, until I hit a ripple and toppled. But Carl had prepared me for that, too: "Get on your belly! Dig in the point of your axe!" No damage followed, and I had learned what to me is one of the exhilarations of the mountains—the glissade when the snow is right.

Who introduced Carl to the glissade I do not know. He began climbing at the age of fifteen or so, at a period when practically every person in the Rocky Mountains thought that any person, especially a woman, who would go up a peak just for the hell of it was more than a little "teched." Because there was seldom anyone around, in Carl's early days, to show him what to do, he and his friends improvised with cumbersome equipment. Some items, like carabiners, were imported, and the Club always had a barrel of Swiss hobs and edging nails around, with the address of a shoemaker who could put them on. Other things were homemade, like Carl's first skis. My brother Dwight, Mel Griffiths, and others forged their own pitons—heavy clunkers they were, too, if you had many to carry.

Often the hardest part of the climb was just reaching the peak. There were neither roads, four-wheel-drive vehicles, featherweight sleeping bags, freeze-dried food, or five-pound backpack frames. So you learned to lash your gear onto a pack horse or donkey and persuade it to follow you through bogs and downed timber—and, believe me, that was improvising!

Carl went through it all. He took his pictures with cameras that had no automatic features whatsoever. Before he was thirty, Carl and Bill Ervin had climbed every Fourteener in Colorado—they were the first known to have done so. He had most of them under his belt before he began climbing, notably in Wyoming, with two experienced alpinists, Albert Ellingwood and Hermann Buhl. They helped him refine his self-taught techniques. I doubt, though, that they taught him his gentleness, patience, and his ability to make others feel comfortable on an uncomfortable cliff. Those traits were inherent, as was his generosity in passing on what he knew about ice axes and all kinds of other things.

Turn the pages. You'll hear his voice. You'll know it's true.

Nothing much of importance on this page.

Our Hero

Not a hell-uv-a-lot here either.

Introduction

By Barbara J. Euser

Carl Blaurock was climbing mountains in the days before nylon rope and factory-made pitons. He was climbing in the days of edging nails instead of vibram soles, in the days of newspapers stuffed in shirts and pants to keep the wind from cutting through, in the days of climbing in ties and tweed jackets.

Carl was born in Denver on April 22, 1894. He grew up there and attended North Denver High School and the Colorado School of Mines, from which he graduated in 1916. His father was a manufacturer of gold and silver products for dentists and jewelers, and Carl, having studied metallurgy at the School of Mines, decided to make that his career. He worked first with his father until the elder Blaurock retired in 1923, and then carried on the business for another half-century, until 1972, before retiring himself. Carl's vocation served to support his avocations—climbing, skiing, and taking photographs.

Adventures

Carl was among the most avid American climbers for more than half a century. As far as anyone knows, Carl and his climbing partner, Bill Ervin, were the first to climb all of the 14,000-foot peaks in Colorado which they did by 1923. They also tried to climb all the Fourteeners in California, but they lacked enough time to capture the last four, and it wasn't until 1957 that Carl alone finally accomplished their goal.

Carl Blaurock atop Blanca Peak.

Carl's climbing career included several first ascents. On a 1924 expedition to the Wind River Range in Wyoming, then the most pristine wilderness, he and his companions, Hermann and Elmina Buhl and Albert Ellingwood, made first ascents of Mounts Helen, Turret, and Harding, the latter now called Mount Warren. In Colorado, however, Carl claims only one

first ascent, that of Lone Eagle Peak, made with Stephen H. Hart. As Carl says, "When I speak of first ascents, I speak of them with a question mark—who knows who's been ahead of you? In 1920, when I climbed the Crestone Needle, I thought we had a first ascent. After I got back to Denver, Francis Rogers heard of our climb and said, 'Well, you know

Ellingwood and Eleanor Davis climbed that in 1916.' But we saw no evidence on the top. Maybe we didn't search hard enough, because I know that in climbing with Ellingwood, we always left a record with a bottle or tin can or something, of our climbs. But, we saw no can and didn't find the record. That and the fact that a rancher down at the foot said, 'Well, as far as I know, the Crestones haven't been climbed,' made us think that we had a first ascent. I know now it was the second ascent."

Climbers were true explorers in the mountains in those days. A climb may have been a first, second, or third ascent; there was often no way to be sure. In 1924, Albert Ellingwood and Carl were only the third party to reach the main summit of Mount Moran in the Tetons, the first party having climbed it only two years before.

On the east face of Longs Peak, Carl narrowly missed first ascents twice in the early 1920s. One summer, a group successfully climbed the east face two weeks before Carl's party made the same ascent. And in the winter of 1924-25, he made two attempts with Agnes Vaille and Walter Kiener. In October, they were turned back by bad weather. In November, the three struggled to within fifty feet of the summit ridge, but faced a blank wall of granite and turned back as night fell. In January 1925, Agnes Vaille and Kiener did make the first winter ascent of the east face of Longs Peak—only to have the climb end in tragedy.

While Carl's nearly seven decades of climbing took him all over the western United States, he does regret that his busy and successful business never allowed him time to climb in South America or Alaska. He did climb the volcanoes in Mexico, and, in 1926, spent six weeks climbing in the Alps.

Equipment

By the early 1920s, climbing was a much more developed sport in Switzerland than in the United States. It was in the Swiss Alps that Carl learned ice and snow techniques. Although he took his first pair of

Climbing pals. Carl Blaurock (l.) and Bill Ervin.

Crestone Needle and admirers.

"Feeture film."

Carl Blaurock on Mount Evans.

crampons to Switzerland with him, he didn't use them there. In fact, Carl didn't use crampons at all until he climbed Mount Rainier in 1939. Instead, he relied on his ice axe and step-cutting techniques—crampons were, in Carl's words, "kind of a nuisance to wear."

Climbing ropes were made of hemp before World War II, and although Carl learned to rappel sometime around 1920, he used a rope more as a hand line than as a belay. Imported from Europe, edging nails provided a great impetus to technical climbing in the 1920s. In fact, it was Carl's friend Hermann Buhl, an accomplished German climber, who immigrated to this country after World War I and brought ice axes and edging nails for sale to members of the Colorado Mountain Club.

Carl's first pitons were custom-made for him by a blacksmith. "I took some ⅜-inch round malleable iron and had an eye bent around at one end of them and the other end hammered into a pointed shape so they could be driven into the rocks. I had half a dozen pitons of that sort made because I hoped to climb Lizard Head Peak, and I knew that we needed long pitons for that. Of course, sometime after I had been to Switzerland, I did have factory-made pitons, too."

When the formation of the Tenth Mountain Division began during World War II, Carl received a nylon rope, piton hammer, and pitons from the War Department with a request to use the rope and give government authorities the benefit of his ideas on how it performed as a climbing rope. Carl found that "of course nylon had great advantage over hemp or cotton rope. It was impervious to moisture and not apt to decay due to wet weather. And the fact that it was elastic was a great advantage." Climbers of the 1980s unanimously agree with Carl's assessment made in the 1940s.

Companions

Over the years, Carl Blaurock climbed with many members of the Colorado Mountain Club and other notable outdoors people, including Albert Ellingwood, Dwight and David Lavender, Stephen H. Hart, Hermann and Elmina Buhl, Agnes Vaille, and his most frequent partner, William "Bill" Ervin. Here is what Carl has to say about them.

Carl's first mountain — Pikes Peak, 1909.

Albert Ellingwood

Albert Ellingwood was an Oxford scholar who learned to climb in Switzerland. After receiving his education in mountaineering there (and graduating from Oxford), Ellingwood returned to the United States and taught economics at Colorado College in Colorado Springs. Carl recalls that "Ellingwood's principle avocation was climbing and he was well-known among the Colorado Mountain Club group in Colorado Springs. He climbed extensively with Eleanor Davis, Bob Ormes, and Steve Hart.

"I was actually only on two expeditions with Ellingwood. One was in the Wind Rivers in 1924 and the other was our own private expedition to the Sierras in California in 1928. Ellingwood had his summers free; so he had lots of opportunity to climb. After he left Colorado, he was an assistant dean at Northwestern University. He died in 1934, but it was quite some months before I heard of it."

Hermann and Elmina Buhl

"Hermann Buhl was a German, and as far as I know, was no relation to Hermann Buhl, the great climber of the 1950s. They both spelled their names the same, but I didn't know of the later-day Hermann Buhl until decades after the Hermann Buhl I knew had died. The man I knew died of pneumonia about 1931. He lived out near Lakeside Park, a block or two away from the lake, and used to go swimming there every day, summer and winter. One winter day he went swimming and caught pneumonia from that and died.

"I think Hermann must have joined the Colorado Mountain Club shortly after he came here, although he was still a member of the Swiss Alpine Club during the years that I knew him. In fact, it was through him that I joined the Swiss Alpine Club when we went over to Switzerland. Hermann thought it would be an advantage to us to be members of the club; so he endorsed our application and I became a member for several years. I finally dropped it because I knew I'd never get back there to climb.

"Hermann's wife Elmina is still living in the same house they built. I called on her last year. She was Denver-born and her maiden name was Wortman. She wasn't an avid mountaineer. I don't think she cared for it too much. The only time the three of us were together on a climbing expedition was to the Wind Rivers, and some of those climbs she didn't make. She seemed to thoroughly enjoy the outdoors and the camping and all that, and wherever we'd take her, she took it all right with ropes and pitons and rappelling, but I wouldn't call her an ardent climber.

"Before our trip to the Wind Rivers, I had heard about that country up there from Arthur Carhart and was immediately interested. While skiing that winter I talked to Hermann Buhl and said, 'I've heard about this Wind River Range, I've got some pictures if you'd like to see them, and maybe you'd like to join us. I'm going to get a crowd to go up there next summer.' I don't remember how I contacted Albert Ellingwood. I knew him and he may have dropped in the office. I knew he had a great desire for climbing and I figured he'd be a good man to add to our group.

"I contacted at least six people. I talked to Agnes Vaille and Agnes was very anxious to go. Bill Ervin said, 'I'd like to do it, but I can't get away.' Later that spring, Agnes told me that her family back East, whom she hadn't seen for a long time, wanted her to come back for a visit that summer. She said, 'I'd rather go with you, but I owe the family a duty of going back there.' I agreed with her on that. I said, 'Agnes, I think you probably should go back and visit your family.' It's a good thing she did because a year from that she was gone. I'm glad I encouraged her to go back East rather than come with us, even though I would have thoroughly enjoyed having her companionship on that trip, too."

Agnes Vaille

"Of the women climbers of that time, Agnes Vaille was a strong, husky woman, just crazy about climbing. She was very personable and a lot of fun to be with. I

"The world is mine." Dudley Smith.

"The set-up."

"The result."

enjoyed Agnes very, very much. The climbs I had with her were mostly on Colorado Mountain Club trips. She and I did take a ski trip into Wild Basin for three days over Christmas in 1923.

"Agnes was born in Denver. Her father, Fredrick Vaille, came from Massachusetts about 1875, and with his brother Howard started the telephone company in 1876. Agnes was secretary to the Denver Chamber of Commerce. She was a very strong-willed woman, very capable, but all in a quiet, unassuming way. Very charming company.

"There were also Lucretia and Gertrude Vaile, but they spelled their name 'Vaile.' Lucretia Vaile was one of the founding members of the Colorado Mountain Club."

William "Bill" Ervin

"Bill Ervin and I were pals in climbing. We climbed all the 14,000-foot peaks together. Once in a while we had another person along with us like Dudley Smith or Bob Nelson, and maybe some other folks, but during the summers of 1921, 1922, and 1923, when we climbed nearly all the 14,000-footers we hadn't previously climbed, it was mostly Bill Ervin and myself, just the two of us.

"Bill was born in Ohio and was ten years older than me. He moved to Colorado as a young fellow and for a while he worked as a bookkeeper. Then he moved to Denver and eventually went in with his friend Albert Platte in the Ervin-Platte Chevrolet Company on Colfax and Gaylord. They later sold out to George Irwin. Bill died of a heart attack in 1943. It was a darn shame."

Of the many people Carl Blaurock climbed with, very few are alive today. Those who are are mostly younger people, such as David Lavender, who Carl remembers teaching to use an ice axe on a climb of Mount Wilson when David and his brother Dwight spent summers on the Western Slope.

Many of Carl's memories are documented with photographs, a selection of the thousands of his photographs forms the basis of this book. Over his climbing career, Carl did a remarkable amount of climbing. Perhaps more important, in his life he achieved a remarkable balance. He established himself as a businessman as well as a climber and photographer. Louise, his wife of almost sixty years, speaks of Carl with obvious pride. Carl Blaurock did not allow his avocations to overpower the rest of his life. Perhaps as a result of his discipline, he was able to sustain his participation in mountaineering for nearly seventy of his now ninety years. And through all the years he has maintained an unfailing sense of humor as an integral part of his pursuits.

Snuggle back into your chair by the fireside and turn the pages. Once again it is 1912, and Carl greets you with a cheery wave and a shout of excitement. "Let's go! It's going to be great up there." Join him on the trail!

William "Bill" Ervin.

"Shorty." Louise Blaurock.

I
COLORADO IN HOBNAIL BOOTS

"Hard-Boiled? I'll Say."

Early Colorado Mountain Club Adventures

Our club, the Colorado Mountain Club, started business officially with a charter meeting on April 26, 1912, with twenty-five people present. Right after it was formed, we set up a committee to schedule trips and outings. We started right in with weekend trips through the summer of 1912. Our first week-long outing was in August up the headwaters of Bear Creek near the summer cabin of the president of the club, James Grafton Rogers. The Rogers family were old-timers in Denver and had this property above the Evans Ranch. Mount Evans, of course, being the high peak in that area, was the main objective of the outing as far fas climbing was concerned.

When we climbed, we carried warm clothing, a sweater, and a windbreak like a jacket of some sort. We didn't have nice nylon and modern windbreaking jackets in those days, like we have today. There were times when I would take newspapers and put them in my shirt as a windbreak and even down my trouser legs to protect my thighs from cold winds. The wind would blow through ordinary cotton or wool trousers or shirts. A leather jacket would stop it, but I've gone up Pikes Peak on New Year's in the bitter cold and have just stuck newspapers in my shirt to protect my stomach and legs from the wind.

This is typical of what I wore—this is an army shirt, those are army britches. At one time I used army fatigues. I was in the army in the First World War, and I came out with a reserve commission so for ten years after that I could go to the Fitzsimmons PX and buy clothing. I preferred the army shoes, and I liked the

army O.D. shirts which were wool. If you get wet in the rain, cotton shirts can get pretty darn chilly whereas wool will keep your body warm. Of course the trousers were tough. That's what I wore clear up until about 1929. I could pick them up for a song rather than going to any of these sporting goods houses for clothes, plus the fact they were efficient and comfortable.

As for sleeping bags, I've still got mine, made in 1912.

They were made for the mountain club by Daniels and Fisher with wool batting and cotton covering. You know, I used that darn bag my whole career except that later on for backpacking I bought a little modern sleeping bag that you roll up in a roll because those old ones were heavy and bulky and awkward. But in the wintertime, I would carry the old heavy bag plus an extra wool blanket.

C.M.C. First Annual Outing — Headwaters of Bear Creek, August, 1912.

Breakfast in camp, August, 1912.

The start for Mount Evans.

Ridge trip, Bierstadt to Evans.

"Hard-boiled? I'll say!" Bill Ervin and Carl.

"A dam-dam-damp night on flanks of old Evans." Timberline camp on Mount Evans, August, 1912.

"Dampened clothes, but not ardor." After the rain, August, 1912.

C.M.C. Second Annual Outing — Main camp near Estes Park, August, 1913.

Loch Vale, August, 1913.

Breakfast in camp, August, 1913.

Summit of James Peak.

"Time to get up." Loch Vale, August, 1913.

Grub carriers.

Mist on Grand Lake, August 11, 1914.

"Ready to move." Fall River trip, August, 1914.

"Three days rain; camp at Lower Chicago Lake."

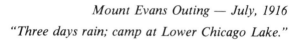

"Oh, what a time!" Lucia Robinson, Sarah Vaille, Jane Bailey, (l. to r.).

Climbing up snowfield on Navaho Peak.

"What a group!"

Summit of Navaho Peak.

"Lunch." Mount Evans, New Year's Day, 1920.

"Bound for the peak."

Summit of Mount Massive with Elbert and La Plata beyond.

Mount Elbert from Twin Lakes.

"The top of Colorado, 14,424 feet."

"Rise and shine." Mount Elbert, July 4, 1919.

"Pleased to meet you!"

"Gee, That Looks Like Real Sport"

Early Skiing in Colorado

In the wintertime, we did a lot of skiing. A lot of climbing, too. On skis, it would take eight hours of climbing uphill, then turn and come back in an hour.

I made my first pair of skis in 1913. We had a four-foot snowfall in Denver, and Carl Howelson came down from Steamboat Springs. He had introduced skiing to the school children and people up at Steamboat right around the turn of the century. Well, he came down and the city built a jump for him out at Inspiration Point in northwest Denver. He did some exhibition jumping there and I went to see it. I thought, "Gee, that look's like real sport! That's for me!" So I went over and looked at his skis. He had eight-foot long skis. Jumping skis have three grooves in them instead of one, so you tend to go straight.

I looked at his skis and made my skis that Christmas vacation at home. I got myself four-inch-by-eight-foot oak boards, and I shaped them into a pair of skis. Made a jib to steam a bend in the front of my mother's washboiler, and I made a set of homemade harnesses and took my summer climbing shoes for ski shoes. I had my foot fixed firmly in the harness that I had developed, and I used that for skiing from 1913 to 1917.

We went up to Estes Park. There was a little ski jump there and we were going on to Porter Lake for an outing, so I decided to try it out. I went down and jumped off that thing and fell and broke my little skis off at the bend, just as we were ready to start on a several-day cross country ski trip! I went to a

"Stand up straight!"

"That's better!"

Snowshoes up, skis down.

blacksmith in Estes Park and had him rivet and shape a piece of iron on the two broken pieces of the skis. That put my kit back into condition where I could use it for the rest of the trip, which I did. I got four years of skiing out of those homemade skis. I wish I had them now—they'd be antiques.

In the old mining days, those miners had homemade skis. They would have one pole and they would ride that pole which was sort of a brake going downhill. I used my poles as a brake, but I didn't straddle them. It was sort of unorthodox, but it worked.

That first year, I walked up the hill on snowshoes. I carried my skis and wore snowshoes up. It wasn't until I met a fellow from Steamboat Springs that I realized you could wear skis both ways. So after that I discarded snowshoes.

I used skins on my skis. The things were actually sacks that fit in the back of my feet or heels of my shoes—you just put one on like a sock over the rear half of your ski and tied it up in front foot. Skins had a disadvantage when you were going over hard snow, but we had a wax that the Haugen brothers—they were a couple of

"Slick 'em up!"

Norwegian fellows who came to Colorado to get in some jumping—made up out of beeswax, turpentine, and rosin. It was a hard wax.

I used that beeswax and rosin mixture clear up to when I quit skiing. I never did fall for those other different types of waxes—climbing waxes, waxes for this kind of snow and that kind of snow.

I always carried my canvas sacks along with me. Climbing a 14,000-foot peak, I'd use those sacks going up, then on top—I'd carry just a plain old slab of

paraffin—I'd rub that on because the hard wax was melted in by then, and then I'd rub the paraffin down with a cloth to shine it slick and nice for the trip down.

George Barnard at the top of the Fern Lake course, 1917.

Walter Carson ready for action. "I'll tell you the old rule we went by—you stand and reach up and touch the tip of your ski. Now they're using shorties for some of this hard pack skiing."

"Every year I'd break a ski jumping off cornices or some darn thing." Our man Carl.

19

Good Times at Fern Lake

"That Fern Lake Lodge was a marvelous place to stage a winter outing. We had a lot of good times up there. Too bad you weren't born then — those were good old days."

"Three Graces — (Oh I guess not Graces.)"

"A real slide."

"A not unusual ending."

"Ditto!"

21

"By the fireside at Fern."

*"One mile to Fern —
Ye gods!"*

Moonlight at Fern Lake.

"Ready for the trail." (Left to right.) Lucretia Vaile, Marjorie Malins, Lucia Robinson.

"Come on!" Alice Hale.

"The snowy look." Jane Bailey.

Marguerite Falls — Winter.

Marguerite Falls — Summer.

"Comin' down the mountain!"

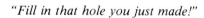

"Fill in that hole you just made!"

Notch Mountain from Bill Ervin's camera.

Ups and downs on the trail to Fern Lake.

The group at Fern Lake Lodge.

"Some of those boards were long!" The crew, 1917.

Ski trip assembly, 1917.

Gentleman Bill Ervin lends a hand.

On the trail to Fern Lake.

"Oh, no!"

"The Closest I Ever Came . . ."

St. Vrain Glacier, July, 1916

I was with George Harvey in his car on the Audubon trip. Part of the gang took the railroad to Ward and some of us went up in cars. That particular trip was the closest I ever came to being killed on a climb. My feet slipped at the top of the St. Vrain Glacier and I slid several hundred feet. That was a narrow escape.

You see, it was frozen snow and all of a sudden my feet went out from under me, I sat down, and there I went. I didn't have an ice axe—nothing. I tried to slow my progress with my heels and elbows, but it was all over so fast. I was fighting to keep my feet ahead of me, so I didn't turn around and go head first.

Fortunately, the lower lip of the crevasse was about six feet below the upper lip. The crevasse was about thirty or forty feet deep. If I'd fallen into it, I'd have hit that wall with a bang. It's the lower part of the glacier pulling away from the rock cliff, see. This is looking at the crevasse itself and this part of the glacier is pulling away from it.

We had come along the ridge and started down here. Part way down we rolled some rocks and they disappeared. From up there you couldn't look into the crevasse because the downhill lip was lower than the upper one. Our rocks rolled past this end of it and went on down onto the face, so we knew that if we worked over far enough, we could slide safely past that spot.

That's what I was trying to do. I was kicking steps along there, but we got in the shadow of the cliff—it was late afternoon—and as soon as you get in the shadow, the snow which is soft enough to step in the sunlight, freezes and crusts. I got careless kicking steps and my feet went right out from under me. I sat down and away I went, right on down and over the crevasse. The fall ran me into the snow up to my waist—snow that ordinarily you didn't sink into over your ankles. I was lucky, too, because there was a ridge of snow there and when I went over the edge of the crevasse, I hit on that instead of falling straight in.

The view south from Sawtooth Mountain.

Mushroom Rock

St. Vrain Glacier, July 4, 1916.   *The crevasse.*

"It Was An Expedition To Go Down There"

Blanca Peak, July, 1920

"A tough gang." Blanca Peak trip, July, 1920.

In those days, more than sixty years ago, it was an expedition to go down to the San Juans from Denver. You couldn't make it in one day. With old Model Ts and old Dodges, it was a couple-day trip clear down to the southwestern part of the state. By 1921, Bill Ervin and I had climbed all of the Fourteeners, using railroads when we didn't use my car. We would go down there and get off the train at Creede and walk over to Ouray and Telluride and climb the peaks in between. That's the way the two of us got all the Fourteeners.

Mount Baldy, now called Mount Lindsey, from the summit of Blanca Peak.

We thought we got the last one in 1921, but I think that that summer they raised one more to a Fourteener, so we went on to climb that. We climbed all of the others that later became Fourteeners—Snowmass and Mount of the Holy Cross for instance—that were not 14,000-foot peaks sixty years ago, but that on later surveys were raised to that elevation. The earlier surveys that go back to the 1880s weren't as accurate as the present-day surveys—either that or the mountains are growing—which is possible too, because I think the eastern part of the United States is sinking and the western part, the Sierras and the Rockies, is rising.

On one trip Bill and I took the railroad and got off at the town of Blanca in the San Luis Valley. Then, we arranged with a fellow in the local garage to drive us into the hills as far as he could so that we could climb Blanca Peak. He also took us the following day down toward the town of San Luis where we were going to climb Culebra Peak. We did that a lot—took the train to the closest town from which we could get our peak, and then either walked in or rented a car or a car and driver. It was very reasonable. The dollar was a different kind of animal than it is today.

Very often, we'd make arrangements with our drivers to have them pick us up again. It might be only a one-day trip, and it might be only a half hour's drive from the city, so we'd say, "See you again at five o'clock," and they would come and pick us up.

Here we are on Blanca Peak. What a crowd! Those moustaches are charcoal that we used sometimes to prevent sunburn. Later, I used rough and lanolin. It made a pretty fair sun cream. But before that it was just charcoal and maybe vaseline so that it would stay on.

"Going down!" Blanca glissade.

"Questionable Characters"
(Left to right) George Harvey, Carl, Bill, Cleon Brown, and Fred Hild.
Elevation 14,390, Summit of Blanca Peak.

"We Didn't Get There Until 1920"

Crestone Needle, July, 1920

Snowbank on ascent of Crestone Needle,.

We thought we had made the first ascent of the Crestones, but later found out different. Albert Ellingwood and Eleanor Davis had climbed it first in 1916. We didn't get there until 1920. But there was no evidence on top and it wasn't until sometime after we got back to Denver that I found out it had been climbed before.

George Harvey and "Good-looking Betty" Burwell.

"Three Queens" — *(Left to right.) Agnes Vaille, Betty Burwell, and Mary Bergen.*

"Oh boy!" Bill and Betty.   *"The Crestone crowd."*

Here are some of the folks on the climb. That's Agnes Vaille and Betty Burwell. This is Mary Bergen—she is ninety years old and living in north Denver. I talked to her just the other day.

We drove down from Denver and hiked up South Colony Creek and camped at South Colony Lakes.

Here's the Arete [Ellingwood Arete on Crestone Needle], and there's Crestone Peak and the slopes of Humboldt Peak on the right. I took that picture from Marble Mountain. I like that. I consider that my best high mountain picture. The pattern of the snow and cliffs and all that. A striking photograph.

Crestone Needle.

"My favorite."

Edge Nails

BY CARL BLAUROCK

A keg of nice sharp Swiss edging nails is now on tap at the Club room. These are just the thing for rough work. They are better than eyebrows when it comes to clinging on cliffs, and will make a pair of soles last at least three times as long as with the ordinary hobs alone. There are nails for every size and shape of foot. Large ones for big-feeted men with heavy soles, medium sizes for medium people, and cute little nails for the ladies' thin soled shoes, also hobnails to go on the bottoms.

A word of explanation for those unfamiliar with their use. An edging nail is made of soft iron, the spike of which is about an inch long and pierces clear thru the sole from the bottom coming thru just outside the welt and is bent over and clinched under the tongue on the head of the nail, the tongue coming over the edge of the sole and thus protecting it from wear. The whole edge of the sole and heel are lined with these nails and the bottoms of the shoes are hobnailed. This protects the whole sole from wear, particularly the edge wear which so quickly cuts the stitching on soles and leaves them flopping. One member of the Club has worn a pair of shoes thus nailed on more than forty high peaks and travel in the roughest kind of country, and the shoes are still fit for tramping. About 100 edge nails are required for a pair of shoes, and the cost is about a cent apiece.

Order a set now and fix up a new pair of shoes for the summer season. Nails will be sent parcel post C.O.D. if you just send your order to Carl Blaurock, 1526½ Champa Street, specifying the size of your shoes, whether heavy soles, and man's or woman's. They add only a few ounces to the weight of a pair of shoes, but are well worth it in the saving of leather and additional security afforded in climbing.

Trail and Timberline, June, 1923

"Could Have Died of Sunlight Poisoning"

Needles Outing, August, 1920

In August of 1920, we went all the way from Denver down to Needleton by train. We had eighty people on the outing for two whole weeks. From Durango north we rode all over the top of the freight cars and everything else.

A pack train took us from Needleton into the campsite about four or five miles up the valley from the railroad. The San Juans being a mountain mining area, there were plenty of pack trains and capable, experienced packers. They're not dude packers like you get in Estes

En route atop the caboose.

Packing in.

Evening in camp.

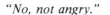

"No, not angry."

Park and some of those places. They know how to tie a double diamond hitch and really pack an animal so that it will stay on.

The first piece of rope I remember using in the mountains was that summer in the San Juans. The rope was just something to hang on—sort of a handhold—climbing some of the steeper snowbanks. If someone slipped in line, the rest of us would hold the rope. There wasn't anything dangerous, just saved them losing a lot of elevation if they slipped and went down. And here, a place like that, the rope could help them when climbing over the rocks. That was the first way we used ropes.

I stood on my head on Sunlight Peak. I thought I would have my feet higher on that mountain than anybody else. Guy beside me was nervous. He said, "You could have died of Sunlight poisoning," and I said, "What do you mean?" He said, "One drop and it would have killed you."

I love the San Juans. The variety of scenery and colorful country is because it is made up of various volcanic formations. It's great country—interesting in so many ways, geologically, the forests, the trees, and even the animals.

At home on Sunday.

"The commissariat." — William Myatt.

"I bid 10 no trump." Grace Harvey (l.) and Nancy Crisp.

"Careful, Betty!"

"Appetite killers."

Minstrels.

"Safety first!" En route to Mount Eolus.

"A long, steep one."

"Please stay in line." Catwalk ridge on Mount Eolus.

"Real mountaineers."

Sunlight, left, and Windom from Mount Eolus.

"Quintessence on Eolus — 14,084 feet."

Summit of Sunlight Peak.

43

Over Columbine Pass.

"High jinks."

On top of Grizzly Peak.

"Scared Cats on a Backyard Fence"

The San Juans, August. 1921

A certain restlessness of feet and a longing to revisit the San Juans was the combination which caused Dudley T. Smith, William F. Ervin, and myself to take a two-week trip in that region in 1921. We left Denver on the Denver and Rio Grande one Saturday evening early in August, each with his equipment of clothes, food, and camera packed in a knapsack, and with well-hobnailed shoes. We planned on making overnight stays either in some cities, or perhaps with ranchers or miners. Instead of camping out and carrying sleeping bags with us for two weeks, we just put up with ranchers or in a mountain hotel or in one instance we stayed in a mine. We had it pretty well laid out so we knew where we would be every day.

The little town of Blanca was our first stop, and from this point in two days we climbed Old Baldy [now Mount Lindsey] and Culebra peaks, then journeyed on by train to the town of Creede. In 1921, we had bad floods in Colorado and Creede was pretty nearly washed out. All the mountain streams as well as the Arkansas River were on the rampage.

From Creede to San Luis Peak and back took two days. We had no place that we knew of to stay the night on that leg of the trip, so we got in touch with a forest ranger and he said the Equity Mine was about halfway between Creede and San Luis Peak. "The mine is shut down," he said, "but the caretaker comes to town about twice a month. I'll see if he'll put you fellows up. I think he probably will."

Little Bear Peak and Blanca Peak above and below the clouds.

Carl, Bill, and Dudley on the summit of Culebra Peak.

Dudley Smith in Creede.

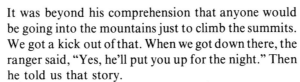

Bill Ervin (l.) and Dudley Smith on Culebra Peak.

When the fellow came to town, the forest ranger said, "There are some fellows from Denver wanting to come down here on such and such a day and climb the peaks around here and they wonder if you would put them up over night."

The caretaker kind of hesitated a little bit, then said, "Frank, you've known me for a long time. Shoot straight with me! What are these men—revenuers out looking for stills?"

It was beyond his comprehension that anyone would be going into the mountains just to climb the summits. We got a kick out of that. When we got down there, the ranger said, "Yes, he'll put you up for the night." Then he told us that story.

We got down there, and he was a very gracious guy. We got right on with him and he seemed to like us. We went out that next morning and climbed the peak and came back that night and, by golly, he had baked a cake and

Carl, Dudley, and the host of the Equity mine.

Bill, Carl, and Dudley atop San Luis Peak.

"On our way!"

had a stew made for us. "It's lonesome out here. You fellows can come stay a week or two weeks if you'd like. I've got plenty of grub here." There are lots of incidents like that. They're the little sidelights you encounter in climbing.

Our schedule then took us cross country to Lake City, part of the time following the Continental Divide across the mountain tops and the rest of the way following the road into town. With this point as a base, we climbed Handies, Sunshine, Redcloud, and Uncompahgre peaks, which gave us a most comprehensive view of the San Juan region.

The view from Handies was the best we had, as this mountain stands in the center of a circle of 14,000-foot peaks, and high, jagged connecting ridges, with broken-up country between, such as no other section of the state can boast. Far to the south lay the Needle Mountains with their delightful memories of last year's outing, then off to the west was the Wilson Peak

View west from Handies Peak of the Wilsons and El Diente.

Lake San Cristobal south of Lake City.

Climbing out of Sherman.

Uncompahgre Peak from the southwest.

Wetterhorn Peak looking west from Uncompahgre Peak.

country with the picturesquely-colored mountains of the Silverton and Ouray region lying between. Farther on to the north were Uncompahgre, Wetterhorn, and a mass of smaller but none-the-less spectacular peaks, while far off on the skyline beyond were the mountains of the Aspen district. Then still more to the east was the Collegiate Range, and just across the San Luis Valley, the noble Sangre de Cristos. I doubt if there is another spot in the state from which so many 14,000-foot peaks are visible, and certainly none can give a more magnificent spectacle of tumbled, jagged mountains.

From Lake City, our route took us up Henson Creek, past Rose's Cabin, across American Flats, and down the precipitous walled canyon of Bear Creek into Ouray. Here an excellent supper and a swim in the hot springs soothed our tired nerves and took the soreness out of aching muscles.

The next day we felt like new men and were ready for our hike over the range to Telluride, part of which was made on horseback. When we got to Telluride that

evening, we were pretty well along on our two-week trip. Our nails were well worn, and our edging nails had gotten particularly loose. So we dropped into a shoemaker's store in Telluride that night and asked the fellow to tighten them. We got to talking to him and told him we were going out the next day to climb the Wilsons.

Leaving there early the following morning, we made a short trip by rail to reach the Wilsons and climbed Wilson Peak the same day. We spent the night in a snug little cabin at about 12,000 feet while the rain drizzled and the snow flew.

With an early start next morning we tackled Mount Wilson and found it the most interesting climb of any. All the ridges of the Wilsons are sharp, loose volcanic rock. The top of Mount Wilson is the high point on one of these razorback ridges and for the last 200 feet, we scrambled along like scared cats on a backyard fence, testing each rock with all our might before we dared trust our weight on it, time and again finding loose

ones which went crashing down for thousands of feet as we pushed them over. But finally, the summit was reached and we paused to enjoy the view, which was poor owing to the thick drifting clouds.

Descending the ridge to the south and sliding over the immense snowbanks lying on the east side, we made our way down Kilpacker Creek through tall grass meadows and beautiful spruce forests to the railroad and back to Telluride. We dropped into the shoemaker's again and told him we had climbed the Wilsons. He didn't seem much impressed.

A year later Agnes Vaille and Mary Crowell, two of our mountain club gals, went on a similar excursion of their own, climbing a couple of weeks in the San Juans just as we had done. They dropped in on this same shoemaker to have their edging nails tightened, and they asked him if many people came in there to climb the peaks. He said, "Last summer a couple of guys came in here and claimed to have climbed 'em!" The gals got a kick out of that. Told us about it. He wasn't

Mount Wilson.

Bill Ervin at Mesa Verde.

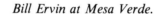

too sure that we'd been able to do it. They went out and climbed them, too.

The following morning we took the train to Mancos and spent one fleeting day in the Mesa Verde ruins, then returned to Denver. Thus ended as wonderful an outing as it had been our lot to enjoy, one in which we had seen the most beautiful and certainly the most rugged mountain scenery in the state. We had traveled

Bill Ervin beneath Mount Wilson with Wilson Peak in the background.

nearly 200 miles on foot, climbed nine 14,000-foot peaks making about 60,000 feet in total elevation, and had enjoyed the hospitality of the great-hearted mountain people and miners in a way which far exceeded our expectations and which is a sure way to revive one's faith in mankind.

Bill Ervin.   **What a pair!**   *Carl Blaurock.*

Agnes Vaille

"For the Night's Campsite We Found A Big Rock"

Christmas, 1922

A warm, cozy rock.

Did I tell you about the time that Agnes Vaille and I went out on a ski trip for two or three days in Wild Basin? We intended to ski over the range to Grand Lake. It was around Christmastime in 1922 and I just happened to see Agnes on the street. "Agnes," I said, "I'm not going to spend Christmas in Denver. I'm going up into Wild Basin on Friday and coming back Tuesday."

"Can I go along?" she asked. "I'd be delighted if you would," I replied.

The two of us went in there and we camped two nights in Wild Basin. The first night we spent at Coburn Lake Lodge. There was just a caretaker there and he put us up. The next day we skiied into Wild Basin, and for the night's campsite we found a big rock. It was slanted and there was a place we could get under. The snow would drift around—you've seen snow in the mountains—the wind will blow it right up against the rock, but there will be a big space between the rock and the snowdrift.

We tramped the snow down, cut a few spruce boughs, and put our sleeping bags down there under that rock. Then we gathered plenty of wood, built a fire up on top of the snow bank, and crawled into our bags. The heat from that rock was so darn hot the first hour that we had to unzip our bags to get comfortable. Then as the fire died down, maybe a couple of times during the night, we put some wood on.

When we woke up in the morning, the treetops were bending, the wind was blowing a gale, and it was

Surveying the route.

wasn't broken through and we bucked that with the car and got stuck and had to shovel through. It took us seven hours to go six miles and get from Coburn Lake Lodge beyond Allen's Park and down into the shelter of St. Vrain Canyon out of the drifts. There was snow all around, but the wind didn't get it and drift it like it did between Allen's Park and Coburn Lake Lodge. We took a snooze in the car—it was her car—she had a little Dodge in those days. She fixed the seat so that it would flatten out backwards. We spent that night in her car after skiing all day and bucking the snowdrifts, trying to get away from that country.

Agnes and Carl.

snowing; so we headed for the divide. We planned to go over it and ski down to Grand Lake. But as soon as we got to timberline in Wild Basin, we couldn't see fifty feet. It was a blizzard, and we didn't dare go ahead. There was also no way to tell whether the pass we wanted to the south of Mount Alice was over here or over there. So we spent the day skiing cross country around Wild Basin, and then went back to our same campsite of the night before.

We spent the second night there and then on the third day came out. We didn't get to the Coburn Lake Lodge where the car was until about six o'clock that evening. In those days the road wasn't even paved and the wind drifts! This was a real blizzard! We came to a drift that

Still moving despite the storm.

Back at the rock.

Carl doing the headstand ritual.

Climbing above Chasm Lake.

At the head of "the Trough."

"Agnes, You're Not Going To Try That East Face?"

January, 1925

One of the saddest events in my life was climbing Longs Peak to help bring down the body of my very dear friend, Agnes Vaille. Agnes had a job at the Chamber of Commerce in Denver. She worked, but she really didn't have to. Her family had been in the telephone business. There were lots of Vailles, and they spelled their names in different ways—Vail, Vaile, Vaille. My partner Bill Ervin used to say there was one "l" of a difference between 'em.

East Face, Longs Peak.

Longs Peak and Mount Meeker across Wild Basin.

Agnes wanted to climb the east face of Longs Peak in the winter—something no one had ever done. She tried first with me and a Swiss fellow named Walter Kiener, an experienced alpinist who had only been in this country a year and a half. We tried it in October, but were turned back by the weather. Then in November, she came to me and wanted to borrow my ice axe for another attempt.

"Agnes, you're not going to try that east face?" I asked. "Don't do it, Agnes! You know how uncertain the weather can be in late fall. I think it's foolish. I wouldn't do it if I were you."

But she persisted, so then I called Kiener and tried to talk him out of it. He was a smart aleck. "Oh, we can do it," he said. "We'll be all right."

So I called Agnes back and said, "Would you object if I went with you. I think the three of us would have a better chance of making it."

"I would sure be glad if you would," she said.

So we three tried it. Instead of crossing the snowslide that comes down from the notch, and which had hardpacked snow below and soft fresh snow on top—we were skittish of avalanches—we took directly up the cliffs on the east side of the notch. We got to within about fifty feet of the summit ridge, but found just a blank wall of granite. We couldn't find a place where we could get anchorage for the climb. We had no pitons, and it was 5:00 in the afternoon and getting dark. So we gave it up. That's hard to do when you're so close to the summit ridge, but we did. We backed off

and got down off the mountain and back to our car about 6:00 the next morning—just in time to drive back to Denver, change clothes, and go to work.

I told them that I wouldn't try it again that fall, but if they would wait till spring—March or April—the difficulty would be as great—more snow—but we would not face the danger of blizzards and winter conditions. I tried to talk them into waiting, but no, they wouldn't. They tried it again in December, and they got part way up the east face when the weather turned sour, and they backed off.

On Sunday, January 11, they were up again. Agnes's friend, Elinor Eppich, stayed with them at the timberline cabin the night before the ascent, but without any intention of climbing. When Agnes and Kiener started out in the morning, Elinor went back to Longs Peak Inn.

It wasn't long before the blizzard hit, but they kept going. Kiener did the step cutting as they went up the notch. He got more exercise during this period than Agnes did, and her hands began to freeze. But Kiener didn't know because she didn't say anything to him about it. They made the summit at 4:00 A.M. Monday morning, but on the way down, Agnes's hands were so frozen that she couldn't hold on. She fell and rolled down the slope and could go only a hundred feet farther. Kiener left her in the shelter of a big rock—as much out of the weather as he could—while he went down to the old timberline cabin to seek help. Being out overnight, he was sure a search party would come up for them.

Sure enough, Kiener met the search party at the timberline house. They had just gotten there a short time before. He hold them about Agnes being up there and Kiener and the three of them started right out to rescue her. They had gone about a half a mile when this one fellow named Sortland, who wasn't dressed for it, just couldn't go any further in the blizzard. He turned back to Longs Peak Inn, but somewhere along the way, he stumbled into a ravine and broke a hip and perished. The snow covered him up and they didn't find him until the next day.

East Face routes.

58

Kiener and the other two pushed on, but about a half mile further, a second man said he couldn't face it, and he also turned back. Then the third man, a woodchopper named Jacob Christian, and Kiener went back up to find Agnes. She had gotten up, taken a few steps forward, and fallen on her face—she died right there.

Then Kiener darn near collapsed; after all, he had been out thirty hours. It was all this other fellow could do to get him back down to the shelter house. But Kiener did not escape scot free. The blizzard cost him all the fingers on one hand except his right index finger, plus he lost all his toes on one foot and half his toes on the other.

Meanwhile, when Agnes didn't show up that night, Elinor Eppich had called her father in Denver, and he called a friend of ours, George Barnard. George called up Bill Ervin and me, and the three of us went up to the rescue. We got to Lyons and called Elinor at Longs Peak Inn. The word had come down that Agnes was alive, but unable to go further because of fatigue. Elinor said that Agnes was all right, she was alive, she couldn't travel anymore, but they had gone back to get her and bring her down. So we thought that if she was coming along all right, there was no use in our going up. So we came back to town. But the next morning there were headlines in the *Rocky Mountain News* that Agnes Vaille had died on Longs Peak.

After that, a group of us from Denver went up to bring the body down, but we had to wait three days because of the blizzard. Then we went up and got the body. I was very fond of Agnes. It was a dirty shame it had to happen.

Roger Toll near where Agnes fell.

Long's Peak across the Boulder Field with "the Keyhole" to the right.

The History of the Wind River Range

BY CARL BLAUROCK

The Wind River Range has a granite core like the whole Rocky Mountain chain in Wyoming and Colorado. Previous to the glacial age these mountains had streams running off in approximately their present valleys.

Then came the ice age, and tremendous accumulations of ice in the high mountains started moving down the stream valleys. This ice may have been 1,000 to 1,500 feet thick, and as it moved it scoured the valleys deeper along with the erosive power of greatly increased stream volume. At the same time the heads of the glaciers started cutting into the ridges between their cirques and as they continued cutting back their cirque walls they would in places cut through the ridges and adjacent cirque walls would touch. Where the ridges were not completely cut through, the remnants of the ridges were left as high, rugged, precipitous peaks which are what we see and climb today now that the ancient ice has melted away. The present ice fields and small glaciers are but the remnants of the last ice age which probably ended 20,000 to 50,000 years ago. At that time the climate became warmer, more like we have today.

Horse Ridge is the remnant of a peneplain that was left because the glaciers moving down the valleys on either side of it did not have sufficient time to cut it entirely away. It is probably the finest example of a peneplain left in the Rockies. In extent it reaches from the Wind River valley at an altitude of around 5,000 feet to the heart of the Range, with an altitude of well over 13,000 feet at its western end. This most unique geological feature slopes upward in a fairly uniform gradient along its entire length of more than 25 miles.

The present topography is due almost entirely to the glacial action. The broad U-shaped valleys are typical of glacial eroded valleys in contrast to the V-shaped valleys of streams. The very large moraines deposited on the floor of the Wind River valley were the terminal and lateral moraines left by the retreating ancient glaciers as they melted in the much warmer climate of the lower valleys.

Trail and Timberline, October, 1946

II
WYOMING WANDERERS:
IN THE WIND RIVERS AND TETONS,
1924

The Wanderers — Carl Blaurock, Elmina Buhl, Hermann Buhl.

August 1

Left Denver 11:30 A.M. and drove through to Laramie, arriving at 8:00 P.M. Lost a lot of time due to three blowouts before reaching Longmont. Roads in general were good. Stopped at Conner Hotel, probably the best. Room $3.50 for two.

August 2

On our way at 8:15 over fairly good roads across lots of desert and sagebrush to Rawlins, arriving at 1:30. Left at 2:30 for Lander where we arrived at 9:30. All rolling country, sagebrush, etc. Crossed old Oregon Trail, went along the Sweetwater, over large flats where road is only a pair of tracks, but good, so that we drove along 25 to 30 m.p.h. The Wind River Range was a rugged silhouette against a gold and orange sky just at sunset. Lander is a good-looking town in a valley of the Popo Agie River, full of green farms, quite a contrast to the intervening country.

First night camp.

Ready to start.

August 3

Met with Arthur M. Cook, the forest supervisor, and Dr. Jones to go over our plans. Later Cook took us out to lunch. Finally left Lander at 4:25 and drove fifty miles to Burnett's Ranch, but stayed at Wertz's place four miles on.

August 4

Waited for Burnett, who was in town, to return and pack us to the mountains. After phoning Cook, we decided to engage Wertz, who then furnished each a saddle horse, packed our duffle on one pack horse and at 11:15 we started. Rode horses seventeen miles in a rather roundabout way up Meadow Creek to timberline (11,000 feet) on the divide between Meadow and Willow Creeks where we camped at about 11,250 feet. Paid Wertz $15.00 and he returned with horses to valley. Mild weather, cooked supper on alcohol stove, had a good night's sleep.

Wind River Panorama — (Left to right.) Knife Point, Fremont Peak, Sacajawea Peak, and Mount Helen.

August 5

Started at 9:15 and soon parted company, each taking the same general direction westerly, heading for the same ridge. A very poor idea as we were later delayed waiting for all to catch up. Followed ridge west above Meadow Creek, climbing until it continued into the ridge dividing North Bull Lake Creek and Dry Creek.

Traversed this ridge which is about a mile wide and without a great loss of elevation in the way of knolls on top, a distance of eight or nine miles from our night's bivouac. Another half mile and we reached Indian Pass, then dropped straight down a broad open couloir with lots of slide rock for about 1,200 feet. We reached

Valley to glacier fields.

North Fork Bull Lake Creek.

a patch of timber at 7:15 and made camp. A very hard day's work as our packs weighing forty to fifty pounds were very tiresome and difficult to handle down the couloir. Had a good comfortable camp and slept well, camp being in Bull Lake Creek Valley.

Looking it over.

August 6

Whole region is very rough and precipitous from glaciation, the valley being full of highly rounded rock formations all the way down as far as we could see. Left camp at 9:15 and climbed up valley towards glacier north of Mount Helen. Reached mouth about two and one-half miles away at 11:30. There is a lake over a quarter of a mile long at the foot with silt practically filling it—laced with milky streams meandering across.

Followed up glacier about two miles or a little more to saddle at head, 12,000 feet elevation and stopped for lunch at 1:45. Continued on at 2:35 and took directly up ridge to summit of Mount Helen. Rough, broken, and steep ridge and chimney. Summit reached at 4:20 and cairn built. Names left in tinfoil in a tin can on summit. Return made over south glacier to camp which we reached at 9:15. Total distance about ten miles.

Mount Helen and glacier.

Enroute to Mount Helen.

Gannett Peak across "vier esel joch."

Ellingwood and Buhl on Mount Helen.

North from Mount Helen.

August 7

Arose at 7:00 and decided to spend day in camp as it was too late to go for Fremont Peak. Washed clothes, loafed, and ate all day. The rest was very welcome. Played cards in afternoon, had supper at 6:30, and retired at 8:30. We like the long twilights we have this far north of Colorado.

Hermann Buhl in camp.

Base Camp — North Fork Bull Lake Creek.

August 8

Arose at 5:00 A.M., had breakfast, and started at 7:00, dropping 700 feet down to Bull Lake Creek which we followed up to the glacier. Many fields of beautiful astors on the way. Found tree cut by an earlier party for a bridge, probably two years ago. Also pole stuck in rocks at foot of moraine. Reached foot of moraine glacier at 9:50.

Fremont glacier field.

Looking over Fremont and glaciers.

Followed glacier to ridge at southeast end of Fremont, then Hermann, Elmina, and self cut steps up ice wall to reach ridge about a quarter mile southeast of summit. Albert took directly up rocks of ridge, but got stuck in a bad place. After the rest of us were on the ridge, Hermann and I backtracked a few hundred feet with the rope to help him up. All finally being on the ridge together, we roped ourselves and continued on to summit over some very rough and steep places. The ridge being narrow and steep on both sides with a number of deep cuts along the way necessitated careful traversing. Finally reached the top at 4:40 where a cold wind was blowing hard.

Signed our names and left them in a tin can with a few rocks piled on top. Could find no other on top, but there was a small cairn at southeast end of summit ridge and a few feet beyond a wooden pole stuck in the rocks. The top itself consists of only the long ridge dropping abruptly on both sides, steepest on the east, and would be more easily climbed from southwest.

Tried descending by following ridge northward, but in a few minutes came to a straight drop of several hundred feet, while on the west it plunged more than 1,000 feet, so had to backtrack to first saddle toward summit from this end which was the head of an ice couloir extending up from the glacier. Could see a healthy bergschrund about 100 feet down, but also knew if we got past this we could slide safely down the glacier below. Cut steps down this ice wall next to the vertical rock wall on about a sixty-degree slope to the bergschrund. It was necessary to lower one person at a time on the rope into the crevasse over a fifteen-foot icicled wall, Hermann letting himself down last on a doubled rope. From here on, the way was easy, down the glacier and into the valley to the south of Mount Helen and back to camp as before in the light of a half moon. Reached camp at 11:00 at the end of a sixteen-hour day.

The ice and snow on the east side of Fremont was black and littered with carcasses of millions of grasshoppers, which probably were blown against the mountain by winds as they attempted to fly across the range.

Blustery summit of Fremont.

Cutting steps on Fremont descent.

67

Albert descending into bergschrund.

With Elmina to follow.

Bergschrund exit.

August 9

Arose about 8:00 and spent most of morning breaking our very comfortable camp, finally getting packed and on our way at 12:30. Started over hill west of camp and followed valley to silt lake at foot of Helen Glacier which we reached at 3:00 P.M. Started climbing here directly up slide under a hot sun. Reached a long snow bank and after that more slide rock to the top of the ridge running east from Mount Harding. [The mountain we called Harding after President Harding is now officially named Mount Warren.] This was the third saddle [now called Blaurock Pass] from the peak and the last one across before reaching Indian Pass above our camp.

This was a long tedious climb of 1,500 feet in elevation with full packs, but at 6:00 we arrived on the saddle at 12,500 feet, then dropped rapidly over slide rock and long snow banks to the Dinwoody Valley. We followed the valley a couple of miles and made camp amidst clumps of timberline Engelmann spruce on a moraine at about 10,300 feet.

Upper Dinwoody glaciers.

This camp was not nearly as attractive as our previous one, being quite rocky and rough with very little grass and flowers. Reached the campsite at 8:00, had supper and retired at 10:30. Mosquitoes were bad, but there were no horseflies as at our previous camp. Distance from first camp about eight miles.

August 10

Up at 8:00 A.M. After a breakfast of prunes, oatmeal, and coffee, Albert and I hit the trail for Mount Harding at 10:00. Hermann had a sore toe and decided to stay in camp with Lou. At 10:45 we were at lake at head of valley and below pass we came over yesterday. By 11:00 we reached foot of first long snowbank between moraine and rock wall and at noon we arrived at end of moraine. Here we headed directly up east side of glacier toward pass at the top.

Hermann Buhl on steep glacier descent.

Turret and Warren.

69

Decided Harding was the mountain east of pass with three distinct tops, the center being the highest. Traveled glacier toward pass until we reached the second couloir this side of pass, then took directly up this, finding it quite steep and with lots of excellent rock work. Started up at 12:40 and reached summit about 750 feet above at 1:40. Congratulated ourselves on having climbed it, then looked across the pass and noticed the other mountain was quite a bit higher and consequently must be 'Harding' and that we were on Turret! In looking up from the base, perspective had fooled us into thinking the one we were on was highest.

We ate lunch of sausage, wheat crackers, raisins, and nuts, took a few pictures and at 2:25 started down toward the pass and found it necessary to use the rope in one place in the couloir. Reached the pass (13,000 feet) at 3:20 and then started directly up ridge for Harding. Good solid climbing first 200 feet, then ridge rose vertical and we crossed to a narrow ledge on south side which became too risky in a few hundred feet, so dropped down fifty feet and climbed up a couloir for about 300 feet which brought us to the southeast side of the mountain.

Fremont Peak from Turret.

Gannett Peak from Turret.

Ellingwood and Buhl on Mount Warren.

Southwest from Mount Warren.

Climbing above Gannett bergschrund.

On Gannett Glacier.

This side is broad and covered with rocks making easy walking clear to the summit. Toward the top the various sides of the mountain come together and form a narrow ridge as on most of the other peaks. Reached top at 4:10 and ate a can of grapes and took pictures. Started down at 5:00, retracing our steps to the pass and thence to camp about 7:00, making a total time of nine hours and eight miles in distance. Built small cairns on both climbs with our names in tin cans under each.

August 11

Up at 5:30 and after breakfast of oatmeal, prunes and coffee got started at 8:00. Followed stream to glaciers south of Gannett Peak. Reached glacier at 8:50 and went directly up glacier toward southeast rock ridge from summit and skirted rocks all the way until we reached the bergschrund about half way up. Crossed this on a snow bridge and found it necessary to cut about a dozen steps in the solid ice above to reach the rocks.

South from Gannett summit.

East Dinwoody Lake.

Stayed on the rocks to the ridge which we followed to the summit. This we reached at 1:15 and found it much larger than previous peaks which are only high points on ridges. This peak drops straight down on the west and north, but the east side is slanted for several hundred feet and occupied by a large snowbank. The snow near the summit was also littered with carcasses of innumerable grasshoppers.

Directly to the west below Gannett lies the largest glacier in the region. It looks to be about four miles long by two miles wide and drains into the Green River. A short way beyond its terminal is the milkiest lake we have yet seen. The day was warm and clear in most directions with some high clouds and almost no wind, so we sat on top two hours studying the map and admiring the views. At 3:25 we left retracing our steps in general back to camp where we arrived at 5:50 with a total of nine miles walked.

August 12

Arose at 5:30 and after breakfast proceeded to break camp and by 11:15 we started down Dinwoody on the right side of the stream. About six miles down it

Summit of Gannett Peak.

became necessary to cross to the left side in order to reach our objective of the day, Dinwoody Lakes. At this point the stream flowed through a narrow gorge about twenty-five feet wide and thirty to forty feet deep, so we proceeded and found a tree on the opposite side which inclined enough to reach from our side. We scrambled across on this and traveled downstream on the left side.

In a couple of miles, we came to marshy flats where the steam from Downs Lake drained in and this gave us some inconvenience and wet feet in crossing. Shortly after, we hit a nicely blazed trail which at about 9,300 feet altitude started climbing up over a ridge, following a dry creek bed most of the way.

In about two and a half miles, we dropped a few feet into a charming valley with a lake in it, the southeast Dinwoody Lake at an elevation of 10,000 feet. This we reached at 8:10 and made camp for the night. The moon came up nearly full and the reflections of cliffs, shadows, light and clouds in the lake was very beautiful. Also mosquitoes and other insects were much less bothersome. Nearly an ideal camp. Made lots of corn cakes to use for dinner next day. Retired at 11:30 after a day's walk of fourteen miles.

August 13

Up at 7:00 and at 11:00 were on our way. Shot a grouse about a mile from camp. Followed a good trail for about five miles and then lost it in the grass, but after hunting a long time found it again and stayed with it across the divide at 10,700 feet to East Torrey Creek.

Passed top at 2:00 and a mile from top on other side passed a corral just at timberline. Lots of cattle and good pasturage at this place. Missed trail here which crosses creek near corral and goes down east side of stream whereas we took the west side following the creek and finding some steep and rough going through cliffs before reaching the bottom of the valley 1,200 feet below at 6:00. Grassy and marshy here and in another mile, we saw a log cut for a bridge across the creek, so went over and found a good trail which we followed to the junction of East and West Torrey Creeks. There it petered out and we looked in vain for its continuance.

Was now 8:00 so made camp and had supper of grouse, soup and cocoa, very appetizing. Nice stand of lodgepole where we made camp. The trail we used is only part of a trail being constructed and instead of using it we should have stayed on right-hand side of creek at upper part and it would have hit a good trail down to Torreys Lake. A short way below the corral, we scared up a lot of grouse, but failed to hit any. What a meal we would have had! Distance today about twelve miles.

August 14

Out of bed at 6:30 and hunted for an hour for trail, but not finding any we threw a log across West Torrey Creek and Ellingwood started across, slipped and in trying to catch himself dropped his ice axe in the stream in the midst of a waterfall. After all were across, he stripped, tied a rope around his waist and went in to hunt for it. After fifteen minutes of vain search in the cold powerful torrent, he gave up looking for it.

We continued downstream through miserable going over rocky formations and fallen willows taking an hour and a half to make about a mile. Finally emerged on good going two miles below junction of creek where sedimentaries joined the granites, and the pines, aspens, and willows gave way to cedars and sagebrush. A mile away and 600 feet below us, we could see a road, so made for it. At end of road reached a homesteader's cabin belonging to Charles Best and a mile beyond that another homestead also belonging to the Best family.

While negotiating with them for a ride in their auto to Boardman's three miles away, Captain Cook and a Mr. Brown drove up in a Dodge roadster, so we enjoyed a reunion. While the rest got ready for lunch, Brown and I drove to Boardman's to get my Ford, then returned

Coming out of Wind Rivers.

Torrey Lake Club folks.

and joined the others at lunch. After lunch, Cook and Brown went up into the mountains to get some weed specimens which had been poisoning cattle, while our group drove to Boardman's, where we were cordially greeted and taken in by the Underwoods of New York. Enjoyed a fine visit all afternoon and being invited to stay overnight, Hermann and I took a bath in the stream and put on clean clothes—a wonderful feeling. A shave afterwards and we felt like humans once more.

About 5:30, the rest of the colony returned from town and we all had supper. In the afternoon we had enjoyed homemade rolls and rhubarb marmalade at Mrs. Underwood's. A nice motherly soul. Met the Voorhies,

Torrey Lake Club.

Mrs. Elmer Underwood.

Mr. Boardman, the Woolerys (camp managers and horse wranglers), and others of the colony including four fine young ladies. In evening all joined around the fireplace in the Voorhies' cabin chatting and joking merrily. Full moon shone beautifully across Torrey Lake. All three lakes are charming in their sagebrush setting surrounded by pine and grass-clad hills.

Retired at 10:30. Have seldom enjoyed such hospitality and cordial welcome as these people showed us. The Boardman colony on Torrey Lake was an exclusive club of easterners who carefully picked their guests and members.

August 15

Arose at 6:00 and breakfasted at 6:30. After visiting a while, finally got started at 9:00 and headed for Dubois, eight miles away. The road was rather rough until we hit the main road which was fairly good.

At Dubois the other three had their shoes repaired and I put in a new speedometer chain. Took till noon to get things ready, so we had a nice meal at Welty's Inn, and at 1:00 were on our way again following the Wind River with its picturesque red, white and buff sandstone 'badlands' and bluffs on one side and pine and grass-covered slopes on the other. The road was good and as it climbed up the valley, the country changed into rolling hills covered with lodgepole pine while the roughly eroded brown and white bluffs beyond, called the Pinnacles, set off the whole very fittingly.

Brooks Lake was reached at 3:00 and is set in a wide valley with the Pinnacles rising behind. Stopped here a few minutes to see the excellent log hotel, then continued on. Road was double width and smooth and we soon reached Togwotee Pass at 9,658 feet and then on and over finally reaching Moran at 6:00. Had a good steak dinner at the attractive log lodge here, wrote letters until 11:00, then turned in. Hotel charge was $1.00 for the meal and the same for a bed.

August 16

Arose at 7:00 and after breakfast had punctures fixed, loaded with gas at fifty cents a gallon and oil at forty-five cents a quart and then drove fifteen miles south from Moran past Jenny Lake to Lucas's Ranch where we left car at foot of mountain. (Elevation 6,900 feet)

Albert, Carl, Elmina, and Hermann leaving Torrey Lake Club.

Started climb at 12:30, working toward Bradley Gulch up which we went to 9,000 feet and found a delightful campsite in a little grassy hollow surrounded by high cliffs, with a little clear stream tumbling down over rocks behind camp and the Middle Teton rising and filling the upper spaces above the waterfalls. Reached camp at 4:00 after a three-mile walk and made camp leisurely. Sat around campfire until 8:30 when we retired in order to be fresh for an early start in the morning.

August 17

Up at 5:15 and breakfasted on Wheaties, prunes, milk, bacon and eggs, pancakes and coffee. Living royally on this mountain! Started at 7:30 and followed up Bradley Creek keeping next to cliffs at right, the last mile being over large boulders to the lower saddle which we reached at 10:15, elevation 11,600 feet. Wind blows hard from west through the saddle. Fine views west from here into Idaho with rough canyons and sedimentary hills. Big glacier in basin directly below,

very dirty. Black dike thirty feet wide cuts clear across the Middle Teton east to west about 200 feet above and south of the lower saddle.

At 10:30 started on to upper saddle, 13,100 feet where we arrived at 11:30. From the upper saddle, cliffs drop nearly sheer 3,000 feet to valley below. We now climbed up our left about 100 feet on a west spur of the

Rail fence and Grand Teton.

mountain where there is an artificial enclosure built up of slabs of stone made by someone years ago, purpose unknown. Here we photographed the west face of the Grand Teton which rises 600 feet above the saddle and up which we would climb. Ate lunch in the enclosure and waited for sun to swing around for pictures.

Dropped back to saddle at 1:30, roped up and started for the summit. My companions put on sneakers, but I kept on my hob-nailed shoes. All cliff work, some very steep, and in one place we lay on our stomachs and crawled along a narrow ledge where you can look down hundreds of feet. This place is known as 'The Crawl.' Reached the summit at 2:30 and found Colgate can with Ellingwood's and Eleanor Davis's names left there on their climb last year. Also a glass mustard bottle, sardine can, and a small can with names of

Above the Lower Saddle, Grand Teton.

Black dike on Middle Teton.

"The Enclosure" above the Upper Saddle, Grand Teton.

Ellingwood on "The Crawl."

Ellingwood standing at "The Crawl."

End of "The Crawl."

"A friendly assist." Ellingwood on Carl's shoulders.

Owen's party of August 11, 1898, in it. Had met a party of eight people descending in the morning as we were climbing up. Geraldine Lucas at whose ranch we left our car was one of them. We found their names on the summit, also a U.S. flag about three by seven feet which they had mounted on the cairn.

Started down at 3:15 reaching upper saddle at 4:30, and stopped to take some pictures. Left in fifteen minutes and reached lower saddle at 5:15 and on to camp at 6:45. Mrs. Buhl did not climb with us. Had supper and sat around a campfire until after midnight.

August 18

Arose at 8:00, had breakfast, broke camp, started down at 11:15 arriving in valley at 12:50. Drove across to Lucas's ranch house, chatted awhile with Mrs. Lucas and a couple of the boys who were on the climb with her, then drove on to Mrs. Johnson's eating place at Jenny Lake and had a nice meal. Went on to the end of the road at Leigh Lake and found an excellent camp spot. This road ends three miles from the cross road to Moran. Reached our campsite at 4:15. Here there was a long sandy beach, so we men went in swimming.

Water was warm and we were much refreshed. Directly across the lake rose Mount Moran, looking magnificent. We made our beds in the lodgepole forest about fifty feet back from the water. After supper we retired early to our comfortable sleeping bags. We knew we had to make an early start in morning for the long trip to Mount Moran.

Carl shaving in camp at Leigh Lake.

Grand Teton summit.

Grand Teton route above "The Crawl."

August 19

Albert and I arose at 5:30, got breakfast, and at 7:20 started for our climb from camp at 6,800 feet. Hermann's infected toe was bothering him, so he didn't go along. We followed the sandy beach a half mile from camp, then took a trail that started at this point and followed the shore in the timber to the north end of the lake where there was a large meadow with a deserted

Ellingwood traverses on the northeast ridge of Mount Moran.

Mount Moran across String Lake.

house. Reached this at 8:45 and then followed the trail still further around some little lakes until it disappeared. We were then in the midst of a tangle of lodgepole, aspens, swamps, and underbrush.

Worked our way through this around base of mountain to the northwest until we reached the valley draining the glacier lying halfway up the peak on the northeast. Cut across this valley over willows, large boulders, and tangled underbrush to the ridge on the western side. We took directly up this ridge which is the northeast ridge of the mountain. Here we found and followed a game trail most of the way to timberline. Elk tracks and droppings as well as trails and beds were plentiful in the valley, and Albert saw an elk just before we reached the ridge.

Arrived at timberline, 9,600 feet at 10:30 and saw a highly broken, shattered, and sharp ridge reaching apparently to the summit. We took directly to this ridge and followed it practically along the top,

occasionally having to drop to one side or the other to get by difficult places. Found excellent, sometimes very steep rock climbing, mostly solid. Some places were loose, but nowhere was it dangerous rock work.

We stayed on this ridge clear to the northern summit arriving at 12:45. The top was about 100 feet wide, comparatively flat, and several hundred feet in length. Ahead of us lay the main summit, about 150 feet higher and a quarter of a mile away, connected by a sharp ridge. Found the names of Jeffers and Joysters in a bottle.

At 12:45, we started for the main summit where we arrived at 1:12, elevation 12,600 feet. Main peak is several acres in extent, more or less flat, and covered with small and large shattered rock. A porphyry dike of brown rock sixty feet wide cuts across the white granite at the southern end, visible for miles across the range to the west and directly down the east face of Moran.

Main summit to go.

Lower summit from top.

Blaurock and Ellingwood atop Moran with Grand Teton in background.

Descending the couloirs off Moran.

Found names of Dr. L. H. Hardy, Ben C. Rich, and Bennett McNulty signed in a Prince Albert tin with date of July 27, 1922. Also added were names of Leroy Jeffers and W. H. Loyster under date of August 22, 1922, so we added our names as probably the third ascent and replaced the tin and glass bottle with names in the cairn.

As the day was cold, sky overcast, a slight breeze blowing, and looking stormy with clouds whipping around the Grand Teton, we dropped down a few feet on the lee side and ate our lunch of crackers, sardines, sausage, Swiss cheese, raisins, and grapes. Far below us lay immense Jackson Lake and all the other smaller lakes.

With the clouds settling lower and a few snow flurries starting with apparent promise of more, we started down quickly at 2:30 and in fifteen minutes reached the lower summit and made for our ridge as fast as possible. Followed our ridge down for a thousand feet until we came to head of a couloir which seemed to lead into the valley directly below the glacier. Here we took to the couloir, which was very steep, but good traveling on the whole, some loose rock but mostly solid.

Finally reached the grassy slopes at 9,000 feet and stopped for water and a short rest. Proceeded straight down grassy slope beside stream and soon came to large morainal boulder beds which we descended. About a mile below the glacier, we found an old tattered sweater and half a mile further a badly weather-beaten and torn air mattress and sleeping bag. We presumed these belonged to Leroy Jeffers whose camp was washed out in a rock slide as per his story in 'Call of the Mountains.'

We followed the stream to foot of the mountain, using game trails where practical, then cut across at base of the mountain, through timber, over logs etc. to the cabin and end of Leigh Lake, thence by our morning trail to our camp where we arrived at 6:50. Enjoyed another bath in the lake, supper, and the campfire. We had quite a shower during the night, the first so far on our nearly three-week outing. Game is very plentiful around the base of Mount Moran and there are numerous beaver ponds.

August 20

Arose at 6:30, broke camp and drove over to Mrs. Johnson's for a fine big breakfast. Heavy white clouds were rolling all over the Teton Range—in fact large cumulus clouds covered the sky in all directions. Drove to Moran, called for mail, then started homeward at 10:50. Reached Togwotee Pass at 1:30 and Dubois thirty-three miles beyond at 3:20. Here we had the pleasure of meeting Mr. and Mrs. Underwood who had come to town for mail. Had a good dinner here at Stringer's Hotel, loaded up on gas and departed at 4:45. Stopped at Lynn Burnett's ranch and visited with him a short while. Proceeded on after dark to Lander where we arrived at 10:15 and went to the Fremont Hotel instead of the Noble and found it a bum place.

August 21

Slept till 8:00, breakfasted, and worked on car, oiling, greasing, watering, and adjusting. Later visited E. H. Fourt at his office for a chat. At noon all gathered with Captain Cook and the Joneses at the Noble Hotel for lunch, after which Doctor Jones and Mr. Fourt drove us to the Indian graveyard where we saw Sacajawea's grave among others. Met the Reverand J. Roberts who runs an Indian girls' school about fifteen miles from town. We next went to St. Michael's Mission (Episcopalian) also on the Washakie Reservation. In the evening all gathered at the Jones' residence for supper and a pleasant bull session. We played the piano and sang afterwards. A most pleasant evening and a good time enjoyed by all.

August 22

Started homeward at 7:00 and arrived at Rawlins for lunch. Proceeded west on Lincoln Highway to Wamsetter and then south to Baggs which re reached at 9:00 P.M. Registered at the Vernon Hotel. Had a nice supper there after which we sang and played the piano much to the amusement of the natives.

Three climbers—three friends.

August 23

Slept well and started over good roads for Dixon at 7:00. Crossed Colorado line and went over Columbine Pass through beautiful wooded country—quite a contrast to Wyoming. Picked lots of chokecherries, bought bread and lunch materials which we ate beside the road overlooking the Yampa Valley. Reached Steamboat Springs in the afternoon and took a swim in the pool. After supper we rode to the top of Rabbit Ears Pass and camped.

August 24

Started after breakfast at 8:00 on the Victory Highway to Grand Lake where we ate dinner at Zicks. At 3:30 we started homeward on the last lap of the trip and reached the Buhls' home at 11:30 where we all stayed overnight. Thus officially ended a most glorious vacation trip of 1,270 miles driving and quite a few miles of hiking and climbing.

Index